making fresh bread

making fresh bread

CREATE FRESH BREAD IN YOUR HOME

WITH PERFECT RESULTS

Love Food ® is an imprint of Parragon Books Ltd

Parragon
Queen Street House
4 Queen Street
Bath BA1 1HE, UK

ISBN: 978-1-4075-4901-9
Printed in China

Designed by Emily Lewis
Photography by Günter Beer
Home economy by Stevan Paul
New recipes by Linda Doeser

NOTES FOR THE READER
This book uses both metric and imperial measurements. Follow the same units of measurement throughout;
do not mix metric and imperial. All spoon measurements are level: teaspoons are assumed to be 5 mL, and
tablespoons are assumed to be 15 mL. Unless otherwise stated, milk is assumed to be full-fat, eggs and
individual vegetables are medium, and pepper is freshly ground black pepper.

The times given are an approximate guide only. Preparation times differ according to the techniques used
by different people and the cooking times may also vary from those stated. Optional ingredients, variations, or
serving suggestions have not been included in the calculations.

Recipes using raw or very lightly cooked eggs should be avoided by infants, the elderly, pregnant women,
convalescents and anyone suffering from an illness. Pregnant and breastfeeding women should avoid
eating peanuts and peanut products. Sufferers from nut allergies should be aware that some of the ready-
made ingredients used in the recipes in this book may contain nuts. Always check the packaging.

contents

introduction

Most people would agree that there are few more appetizing smells than that of freshly baked bread. A better-kept secret, however, is that rhythmically kneading bread dough is a fabulous stress-buster. Making and baking your own bread is a genuinely pleasurable and satisfying activity with the bonus of delicious edible results.

Of course, these days there are bread machines available that will do all the work for you and bake the loaf as well. In light of this, it might seem that making bread by hand and baking it in a conventional oven is rather like reinventing the wheel. Quite apart from the feel-good factor of home-baking, the answer to this criticism is that bread machines are all very well but have their limitations. Only a proportion of the different kinds of bread – never mind the hundreds of different shapes – can be made satisfactorily in a bread machine. They certainly have their uses but will never completely replace the keen and enthusiastic baker, whether a knowledgeable professional or an eager amateur.

It is a mistake to think that making bread dough is time-consuming, although it is true that the process cannot be rushed. What might be described as hands-on time, when you are actively mixing, kneading or shaping the dough, is probably only about 30 minutes, but these activities are separated by much longer periods while the dough is resting or rising. So although several hours may elapse between starting and finishing the process, for quite a lot of that time you are not required in the kitchen and can get on with some other task or watch your favourite television programme.

A WORD ABOUT INGREDIENTS

Given that bread is such a basic staple, it should be no surprise that the ingredients used to make it are found in most kitchens most of the time. As they are so familiar, there is little purpose in repeating information that everyone already knows. However, there are a couple of particular points, and some guidance about cooking with yeast is given on page 8.

Flour is probably the most important ingredient. Strong bread flour, whether white, brown or whole-meal, is most commonly used in yeast doughs. It is milled from hard wheat containing a high level of

the protein gluten, which is what gives the bread its texture. There is no substitute. Plain and self-raising flour are mainly used for teabreads. Of course, not all breads are made from wheat flour. Other grains, including rye, cornmeal, buckwheat, barley and oats, feature in bread recipes all over the world.

Much has been written recently about dangerously high levels of salt in the diet and commercially produced bread has been named as one of the main culprits. Salt is not just added to the dough for additional flavour, although without any salt bread would taste extremely bland. Salt has a retardant effect on yeast – it slows down fermentation. Given that you are always told to leave the dough in a warm place to speed up rising, this might seem an odd thing to recommend. However, because salt regulates the rate of fermentation, the gluten is strengthened, preventing the dough from over-rising and collapsing. It is important, therefore, that you do not omit or reduce the quantity of salt specified in the recipes. Salt substitutes are not effective.

ALL ABOUT YEAST

Yeast is a microscopic fungus used as a raising agent in the doughs of some breads and cakes. When mixed with flour and liquid, it ferments and gives off the gas carbon dioxide which causes the dough to rise. It is a living organism and so can be killed if handled wrongly. It functions most efficiently at a temperature of 21–36°C/70–97°F and this is why recipes emphasize that liquids added to the mixture should be lukewarm and the dough should be left to rise in a warm place. However, temperatures higher than this range will kill the yeast and the dough will never rise. Many people are slightly nervous about using yeast and are confused because it is available in different forms. In fact, it is very easy to distinguish between the three common types of culinary yeast available and to use any of them.

Fresh yeast, sometimes called compressed yeast, is firm, moist and creamy beige in colour. Nowadays it is quite difficult to obtain but may be available from health food shops and baker's suppliers.

It can be stored for up to 2 weeks in the refrigerator. First, put it into a plastic container with a lid and punch a few holes in the lid. To activate fresh yeast, use a fork to mash it with the lukewarm liquid specified in the recipe in a bowl. A pinch of sugar may be added. Once it has formed a smooth paste, add it to the well in the centre of the dry ingredients.

Dried yeast in the form of light brown, medium-size granules is widely available in supermarkets. Although it will keep for a very long time, it is sensible to note the 'use by' date on the packet. If you do use it after this date, make sure that it is frothy before adding it to the other ingredients. To activate dried yeast, mix a teaspoon of sugar with the lukewarm liquid specified in the recipe in a bowl. Sprinkle the yeast over the surface and leave to stand for 10–15 minutes, until frothy. Stir to a paste and add to the well in the centre of the dry ingredients.

Easy-blend dried yeast in the form of fine granules is available from supermarkets and grocers. It is sold in packets containing a number of sachets, each weighing about 7 g/$^1/_4$ oz, the equivalent of 2$^1/_2$ teaspoons. It is the most popular type of yeast and features in many of the recipes in this book. Store it in a cool dry place and take note of the 'use by' date. Easy-blend dried yeast is simply added to the mixture with the flour and the other dry ingredients and does not require activating in advance.

To all intents and purposes, there is little qualitative difference between these yeasts apart from their convenience and availability. However, professionals will often insist that fresh yeast always produces the best bread, and it does have a more distinctive yeasty flavour that some people like. There is a quantitative difference and these are the equivalents (quantities required for 500 g/1 lb 2 oz flour): 15–25 g/$^1/_2$–1 oz fresh yeast = 2 tsp dried yeast = 1 sachet easy-blend dried yeast.

HOW TO KNEAD

Kneading is the process that releases the gluten in the flour to produce a smooth and elastic dough. Once a stiff, sticky dough has been mixed in the bowl, turn it out on to a lightly floured surface and gather it into a ball. Flatten and fold one half over the other, bringing the top towards you. If you are right-handed, push the dough away from you with the heel of your right hand and rotate the dough slightly towards with you with your left hand. Continue to fold the dough, push it with the heel of your hand and rotate it slightly for 10 minutes, until it is smooth and elastic. If you are left-handed, use the heel of your left hand to push the dough and your right hand to rotate it. Stop kneading once the dough is smooth – you'll probably be glad to because it's quite hard work. Over-kneading results in bread with an uneven or very open texture.

Once the dough has doubled in volume, it is knocked back. To do this, punch it with your fist to disperse the gas bubbles produced by the yeast.

TOP TIPS FOR THE BEST BREAD

Generally speaking, making bread is astonishingly easy, although there are some specialist breads that are best left to professionals. It's mostly a matter of common sense and following a few important guidelines.

• Before you start, make sure that you have all the ingredients listed and don't try using substitutes until you've gained a bit of experience.

• Always check the 'use-by' date, particularly on flour because it can become rancid and on yeast because it loses its potency over time.

• Have all ingredients at room temperature before you start. Liquids for yeast doughs should be lukewarm, that is, just hand-hot. If they're any hotter, they will kill the yeast and the dough will not rise.

• Do not try to rush any of the stages, whether kneading or rising (also known as proving) as the results will be disappointing. However, there are some tried-and-tested short-cuts (see page 10).

• A yeast dough will rise more rapidly in a warm place, such as an airing cupboard or the warming drawer of a stove, but do not put the dough somewhere hot, such as directly over a radiator or next to a hot water tank, because you will kill the yeast. A yeast dough will still rise in a cooler place, even in the refrigerator – it just takes longer. If the dough has been left to rise in the refrigerator, which takes about 24 hours, leave it to stand at room temperature for 30 minutes before shaping.

• It is important to cover the dough when it is left to rise to ensure that it rises at a steady rate.

• Once the dough has doubled in volume, knock it back and shape it into a loaf. If it is left to rise for too long, the bread may develop a greyish crumb, smell strongly of yeast and have a heavy feel to it.

• When shaping the dough, flour the work surface only lightly. The dough should not be sticky at this stage and too much flour will spoil the colour of the crust.

• As raising agents such as bicarbonate of soda and baking powder are activated as soon as liquid is

added to the mixture, non-yeast breads should be baked as soon as the loaves are ready and not left standing for prolonged periods.

• Most bread, especially loaves made with yeast dough, should be left to cool on a wire rack for at least 30 minutes before slicing to allow the steam to escape.

• Cut bread with a long, sharp serrated knife, using a sawing action to avoid damaging the delicate crumb. Stand the bread on a wooden board to avoid damaging the knife.

• Freshly baked bread should be stored in a cool dry place, but not in the refrigerator as it will go stale more quickly. Ideally, eat it within 2 days. Some breads and rolls can be frozen, sealed in a freezer bag, for up to 3 months. However, very crusty breads tend to fall apart when thawed.

THE SECRET OF AN EXTRA CRISP CRUST
Brushing the loaf with a salt water glaze before baking and again halfway through helps produce a crisper crust. To make it, mix a pinch of salt with 2 tablespoons of water in a bowl.

Introducing steam into the oven during baking first softens the dough and then enhances caramelization of the sugars in it, producing a crisper crust. The best way to do this is to use a spray bottle to mist the walls, floor and door of the oven with water several times during the first 10 minutes of baking. Make sure that you do not spray the heating elements, fan or oven light. Alternatively, you can simply wipe a damp cloth over the walls, floor and door of the oven, taking care to avoid burning your hand. A third option is to half-fill a roasting tin with water and put it into the base of the oven. Try one of these techniques with rustic breads, such as ciabatta.

Using a baking stone is another way to help create an extra crisp crust, as it has some of the same effect as cooking in a clay or brick oven. It is a thick, unglazed ceramic slab that will draw out moisture from the base of bread placed directly on it. It is mainly used for rustic breads and pizzas. Unglazed terracotta tiles make a good substitute. The stone or tiles should be preheated in the oven for about 30 minutes before the bread is placed directly on top. A peel – a sort of long-handled shovel used by bakers and pizza cooks – is the safest way to do this.

SHORTCUTS
• *Using a bread machine* Available in a number of sizes, these machines take all the work out of making bread. They may be used for mixing the dough, controlling its temperature while rising and for baking the loaf. The size and shape of the pan in the bread machine limits the choice of loaf you can make. However, it can be useful to use the machine for mixing, kneading and rising before turning out the dough and shaping it by hand to bake in the oven. Bread machines are quite large and take up storage space in the kitchen. Some are very expensive. The texture of the bread is softer than that of hand-made loaves. If you are going to use a

bread machine, read the manufacturer's instructions carefully first.

• *Kneading with a mixer or food processor* An electric mixer fitted with one or more dough hooks or a good-quality food processor speeds up the kneading process and reduces the effort involved.

• *Rising in the microwave* When the dough has been kneaded and become smooth and elastic, shape it into a ball and put it into a microwave-proof bowl without oiling it first. Cover with lightly oiled clingfilm and heat on high for 10 seconds, then leave to stand for 20 minutes. If the dough has not doubled in volume, heat on high for a further 10 seconds and leave to stand for a further 10 minutes.

THE FINAL KEY TO SUCCESSFUL BREAD-MAKING

All cooking, including bread-making, is a combination of science and art. Measuring the ingredients, preheating the oven, even following the method in a recipe is the science part. The art aspect comes from getting to know instinctively just how the dough should feel when you knead it or recognizing when the colour and crispness of the crust exactly match the softness of the interior crumb.

Making bread may be affected by lots of variables, such as the temperature and humidity in the kitchen. Samples from two bags of the same brand of flour – never mind a variety of brands – may absorb different amounts of liquid. Learn to trust your senses and your instincts and, in no time, you will 'just know' when the dough needs another spoonful of water or an extra sprinkling of flour to make the truly perfect loaf. And that's something a bread machine will never be able to do.

basic bread recipe

You can make two small loaves or one large loaf with this classic recipe or even shape the dough into about 12 rolls. For other variations, see right.

MAKES 1 LARGE LOAF

Ingredients

500 g/1 lb 2 oz strong white bread flour,
plus extra for dusting
2 tsp salt
1 sachet easy-blend dried yeast
15 g/1/2 oz butter
300 ml/10 fl oz lukewarm water
vegetable oil, for brushing
pinch of salt dissolved in 2 tbsp water, to glaze

1 Sift the flour and salt together into a bowl and stir in the yeast. Add the butter and rub in with your fingertips. Make a well in the centre and pour in the lukewarm water. Stir well with a wooden spoon until the dough begins to come together, then knead with your hands until it leaves the side of the bowl. Turn out on to a lightly floured surface and knead well for about 10 minutes, until smooth and elastic.

2 Brush a bowl with oil. Shape the dough into a ball, put it into the bowl and put the bowl in a plastic bag or cover with a damp tea towel. Leave to rise in a warm place for 1–2 hours, until the dough has doubled in volume.

3 Brush a 19 x 12 x 9-cm/7½ x 4½ x 3½-in loaf tin with oil. Turn out the dough on to a lightly floured surface and knock back with your fist. Leave to rest for 10 minutes, then with a lightly floured hand, flatten the dough into a rectangle the same width as the tin. Fold it into 3 and place in the prepared tin, seam side down. Put the tin into a plastic bag or cover with a damp tea towel and leave to rise in a warm place for 40–80 minutes, until the dough has reached the top of the tin.

4 Meanwhile, preheat the oven to 230°C/450°F/Gas Mark 8. Brush the top of the loaf with the salt water glaze and bake for about 40 minutes, until it has shrunk from the sides of the tin, the crust is golden brown and the loaf sounds hollow when tapped on the base with your knuckles. Turn out on to a wire rack to cool.

COOK'S TIP

If making 2 small loaves, bake for about 30 minutes. Bake rolls on a lightly oiled baking sheet spaced 2.5 cm/1 in apart for 12–15 minutes.

VARIATIONS

- *Wholemeal Bread* Substitute strong wholemeal flour for half the white flour. You may need a little extra lukewarm water. This makes a nutty-flavoured loaf that is not too chewy. If you want to use all wholemeal flour and not a mixture of wholemeal and white flour, add enough water to make a sticky dough and beat well with a wooden spoon. Bake the loaf for 10–20 minutes longer.
- *Basic Brown Bread* Simply substitute brown flour for the white. You may need a little more water to make a smooth dough. This produces a full-flavoured loaf with a denser texture than white bread but lighter than wholemeal.
- *Crown Loaf* Make half the quantity of dough as described in step 1 and leave to rise as described in step 2. Brush a 15-cm/6-in diameter cake tin with oil. Knock back the dough and divide it into 6 pieces. Shape each into a roll and place 5 of them in a ring around the prepared tin. Put the remaining roll in the centre. Put the tin into a plastic bag or cover with a damp tea towel and leave to rise in a warm place for 30 minutes. Meanwhile, preheat the oven to 230°C/450°F/Gas Mark 8. Beat together 1 egg, 1 tbsp water and a pinch of sugar in bowl and brush the glaze over the loaf. Bake for 25–30 minutes.
- *Full-fat Milk Bread* Substitute lukewarm semi-skimmed or full-cream milk for the water, depending on how rich you want the loaf to taste.
- *Enriched Bread* Lightly beat together 1 egg and 1 egg yolk in a measuring jug, then add lukewarm water to make the liquid up to 300 ml/10 fl oz. Add to the dry ingredients and continue as described in the basic recipe.
- *Seed-topped Loaf* Just before baking the bread, brush the top with 1 tbsp milk instead of the salt water glaze and sprinkle with 2 tbsp seeds, such as poppy, sunflower, nigella, sesame, pumpkin, linseed or a mixture.

traditional bread

english muffins

Ingredients

450 g/1 lb strong white bread flour, plus extra for dusting

½ tsp salt

1 tsp caster sugar

1½ tsp easy-blend dried yeast

250 ml/9 fl oz lukewarm water

125 ml/4 fl oz natural yogurt

vegetable oil, for brushing

40 g/1½ oz semolina

MAKES 10–12 MUFFINS

1 Sift the flour and salt together into a bowl and stir in the sugar and yeast. Make a well in the centre and add the lukewarm water and yogurt. Stir with a wooden spoon until the dough begins to come together, then knead with your hands until it comes away from the side of the bowl. Turn out on to a lightly floured surface and knead for 5–10 minutes, until smooth and elastic.

2 Brush a bowl with oil. Shape the dough into a ball, put it in the bowl and put the bowl into a plastic bag or cover with a damp tea towel. Leave to rise in a warm place for 30–40 minutes, until the dough has doubled in volume.

3 Dust a baking sheet with flour. Turn out the dough on to a lightly floured surface and knead lightly. Roll out to a thickness of 2 cm/¾ in. Stamp out 10–12 rounds with a 7.5-cm/3-in biscuit cutter and sprinkle each round with semolina. Transfer the muffins to the prepared baking sheet, put it into a plastic bag or cover with a damp tea towel and leave to rise in a warm place for 30–40 minutes.

4 Heat a griddle or large frying pan over a medium-high heat and brush lightly with oil. Add half the muffins and cook for 7–8 minutes on each side, until golden brown. Cook the remaining muffins in the same way.

5 To serve, split the muffins in half and toast lightly. Alternatively, leave to cool and store in an airtight container for up to 2 days.

brioche

Ingredients

225 g/8 oz strong white bread flour, plus extra for dusting

½ tsp salt

1 tbsp caster sugar

1½ tsp easy-blend dried yeast

2 eggs

2 tbsp lukewarm milk

55 g/2 oz unsalted butter, softened, plus extra for greasing

glaze

1 egg yolk

1 tbsp milk

MAKES 1 LOAF

1 Sift the flour and salt into a food processor and add the sugar and yeast. Lightly beat the eggs with the milk in a bowl. With the machine running, gradually add the egg and milk mixture and process, scraping down the sides as necessary, for 2–3 minutes, until a dough forms. Cut the butter into small pieces and add to the dough. Pulse the machine until the butter is fully incorporated.

2 Grease a bowl with butter. Shape the dough into a ball, put it in the bowl and put the bowl into a plastic bag or cover with a damp tea towel. Leave to rise in a warm place for 1 hour, until the dough has doubled in volume.

3 Grease a brioche tin with butter. Turn out the dough on to a lightly floured surface and knock back gently with your fist. Cut off about one-quarter of the dough and wrap in clingfilm. Knead the larger piece of dough, shape into a ball, place in the prepared tin and indent the top. Unwrap the smaller piece of dough, knead lightly into a pear shape and place on top of the indent to make the tête. Put the tin into a plastic bag or cover with a damp tea towel and leave to rise in a warm place for 1 hour.

4 Preheat the oven to 220°C/425°F/Gas Mark 7. To make the glaze, beat the egg yolk with the milk, then brush over the top of the brioche. Bake for 40–45 minutes, until golden brown. Turn out on to a wire rack to cool.

bagels

Ingredients

350 g/12 oz strong white bread flour, plus extra for dusting

2 tsp salt

1 sachet easy-blend dried yeast

1 tbsp lightly beaten egg

200 ml/7 fl oz lukewarm water

vegetable oil, for brushing

1 egg white

2 tsp water

2 tbsp caraway seeds

MAKES 10 BAGELS

1 Sift the flour and salt together into a bowl and stir in the yeast. Make a well in the centre, pour in the egg and lukewarm water and mix to a dough. Turn out on to a lightly floured surface and knead well for about 10 minutes, until smooth.

2 Brush a bowl with vegetable oil. Shape the dough into a ball, place it in the bowl and put the bowl into a plastic bag or cover with a damp tea towel. Leave to rise in a warm place for 1 hour, until the dough has doubled in volume.

3 Brush 2 baking sheets with oil and dust a tray with flour. Turn out the dough on to a lightly floured surface and knock back with your fist. Knead for 2 minutes, then divide into 10 pieces. Shape each piece into a ball and leave to rest for 5 minutes. Gently flatten each ball with a lightly floured hand and make a hole in the centre with the handle of a wooden spoon. Put the bagels on the floured tray, put the tray in a plastic bag or cover with a damp tea towel and leave to rise in a warm place for 20 minutes.

4 Meanwhile, preheat the oven to 220°C/425°F/Gas Mark 7 and bring a large pan of water to the boil. Lower the heat until the water is barely simmering, then add 2 bagels. Poach for 1 minute, then turn over and poach for a further 30 seconds. Remove with a slotted spoon and drain on a tea towel. Poach the remaining bagels in the same way.

5 Transfer the bagels to the prepared baking sheets. Beat the egg white with the water in a bowl and brush it over the bagels. Sprinkle with the caraway seeds and bake for 25–30 minutes, until golden brown. Transfer to a wire rack to cool.

cottage loaf

Ingredients

675 g/1 lb 8 oz strong white bread flour, plus extra for dusting

2 tsp salt

1 sachet easy-blend dried yeast

400 ml/14 fl oz lukewarm water

vegetable oil, for brushing

MAKES 1 LARGE LOAF

1 Sift the flour and salt together into a bowl. Add the yeast and stir in. Make a well in the centre, pour in the lukewarm water and stir with a wooden spoon until the dough begins to come together, then knead with your hands until it leaves the side of the bowl. Turn out on to a lightly floured surface and knead for about 10 minutes, until smooth and elastic.

2 Brush a bowl with oil. Shape the dough into a ball, put it in the bowl and put the bowl into a plastic bag or cover with a damp tea towel. Leave to rise in a warm place for 1–2 hours, until the dough has doubled in volume.

3 Brush 2 baking sheets with oil. Turn out the dough on to a lightly floured surface and knock back with your fist. Knead for 2 minutes, then divide the dough into 2 pieces, one about twice the size of the other. Shape each piece into a ball, put them on to the prepared baking sheets and put the baking sheets into plastic bags or cover with damp tea towels. Leave to rise in a warm place for 30 minutes.

4 With a floured hand, gently flatten the larger ball of dough. Cut a 5-cm/2-in cross in the centre of the top and brush with water. Put the smaller ball of dough on top. Make small vertical slashes all around both pieces of dough. Brush the handle of a wooden spoon with the oil and push it into the centre of the loaf so that it makes a hole through both pieces of dough. Put the loaf on the baking sheet into a plastic bag or cover with a damp tea towel. Leave in a warm place for 15 minutes.

5 Meanwhile, preheat the oven to 220°C/425°F/Gas Mark 7. Bake the loaf for 40 minutes, until the crust is golden brown and it sounds hollow when tapped on the base with your knuckles. Transfer to a wire rack to cool.

mixed seed bread

Ingredients

375 g/13 oz strong white bread flour, plus extra for dusting

125 g/4½ oz rye flour

1½ tbsp skimmed milk powder

1½ tsp salt

1 tbsp light brown sugar

1 tsp easy-blend dried yeast

1½ tbsp sunflower oil, plus extra for greasing

2 tsp lemon juice

300 ml/10 fl oz lukewarm water

1 tsp caraway seeds

½ tsp poppy seeds

½ tsp sesame seeds

topping

1 egg white

1 tbsp water

1 tbsp sunflower seeds or pumpkin seeds

MAKES 1 MEDIUM LOAF

1 Place the flours, milk powder, salt, sugar and yeast in a large bowl. Pour in the oil and add the lemon juice and water. Stir in the seeds and mix well to make a smooth dough. Turn out on to a lightly floured surface and knead well for about 10 minutes, until smooth.

2 Brush a bowl with oil. Shape the dough into a ball, place it in the bowl and put the bowl into a plastic bag or cover with a damp tea towel. Leave to rise in a warm place for 1 hour, until the dough has doubled in volume.

3 Oil a 900-g/2-lb loaf tin. Turn the dough out on to a lightly floured surface and knead for 1 minute until smooth. Shape the dough the length of the tin and three times the width. Fold the dough into three length-ways and place it in the tin with the join underneath. Cover and leave in a warm place for 30 minutes until it has risen above the tin.

4 Preheat the oven to 220°C/425°F/Gas Mark 7. For the topping, lightly beat the egg white with the water to make a glaze. Just before baking, brush the glaze over the loaf, then gently press the sunflower seeds or pumpkin seeds all over the top.

5 Bake in the oven for 30 minutes, or until firm and golden brown. Test that the loaf is cooked by tapping on the base with your knuckles – it should sound hollow. Transfer to a wire rack to cool.

crusty white bread

Ingredients

1 egg

1 egg yolk

lukewarm water, as required

500 g/1 lb 2 oz strong white bread flour, plus extra for dusting

1½ tsp salt

2 tsp sugar

1 tsp easy-blend dried yeast

25 g/1 oz butter, diced

sunflower oil, for greasing

MAKES 1 MEDIUM LOAF

1 Place the egg and egg yolk in a jug and beat lightly to mix. Add enough lukewarm water to make up to 300 ml/10 fl oz. Stir well.

2 Place the flour, salt, sugar and yeast in a large bowl. Add the butter and rub it in with your fingertips until the mixture resembles breadcrumbs. Make a well in the centre, add the egg mixture and work to a smooth dough.

3 Turn out on to a lightly floured surface and knead well for about 10 minutes, until smooth. Brush a bowl with oil. Shape the dough into a ball, place it in the bowl and put the bowl into a plastic bag or cover with a damp tea towel. Leave to rise in a warm place for 1 hour, until the dough has doubled in volume.

4 Oil a loaf tin. Turn the dough out on to a lightly floured surface and knead for 1 minute until smooth. Shape the dough the length of the tin and three times the width. Fold the dough into three lengthways and place it in the tin with the join underneath. Cover and leave in a warm place for 30 minutes until it has risen above the tin.

5 Preheat the oven to 220°C/425°F/Gas Mark 7. Bake in the oven for 30 minutes, or until firm and golden brown. Test that the loaf is cooked by tapping on the base with your knuckles – it should sound hollow. Transfer to a wire rack to cool.

wholemeal harvest bread

Ingredients

225 g/8 oz strong wholemeal bread flour, plus extra for dusting

1 tbsp skimmed milk powder

1 tsp salt

2 tbsp soft brown sugar

1 tsp easy-blend dried yeast

1½ tbsp sunflower oil, plus extra for greasing

175 ml/6 fl oz lukewarm water

MAKES 1 SMALL LOAF

1 Place the flour, milk powder, salt, sugar and yeast in a large bowl. Pour in the oil and add the water, then mix well to make a smooth dough.

2 Turn out on to a lightly floured surface and knead well for about 10 minutes, until smooth. Brush a bowl with oil. Shape the dough into a ball, place it in the bowl and put the bowl into a plastic bag or cover with a damp tea towel. Leave to rise in a warm place for 1 hour, until the dough has doubled in volume.

3 Oil a 900-g/2-lb loaf tin. Turn the dough out on to a lightly floured surface and knead for 1 minute until smooth. Shape the dough the length of the tin and three times the width. Fold the dough into three lengthways and place it in the tin with the join underneath. Cover and leave in a warm place for 30 minutes until it has risen above the tin.

4 Preheat the oven to 220°C/425°F/Gas Mark 7. Bake in the oven for 30 minutes, or until firm and golden brown. Test that the loaf is cooked by tapping on the base with your knuckles – it should sound hollow. Transfer to a wire rack to cool.

irish soda bread

Ingredients

450 g/1 lb plain flour
1 tsp salt
1 tsp bicarbonate of soda
400 ml/14 fl oz buttermilk

MAKES 1 LOAF

1 Preheat the oven to 220°C/425°F/Gas Mark 7.

2 Sift the flour, salt and bicarbonate of soda into a mixing bowl.

3 Make a well in the centre of the dry ingredients and pour in most of the buttermilk.

4 Mix well together using your hands. The dough should be very soft but not too wet. If necessary, add the remaining buttermilk.

5 Turn the dough out on to a lightly floured surface and knead it lightly. Shape into a 20-cm/8-inch round.

6 Place the bread on a greased baking tray, cut a cross in the top and bake in the oven for 25–30 minutes. Test that the loaf is cooked by tapping on the base with your knuckles – it should sound hollow.

hamburger buns

Ingredients

450 g/1 lb strong white bread flour, plus extra for dusting

1½ tsp salt

2 tsp caster sugar

1 tsp easy-blend dried yeast

150 ml/5 fl oz lukewarm water

150 ml/5 fl oz lukewarm milk

vegetable oil, for brushing

2–3 tbsp sesame seeds

MAKES 8 BUNS

1 Sift the flour and salt together into a bowl and stir in the sugar and yeast. Make a well in the centre and pour in the lukewarm water and milk. Stir well with a wooden spoon until the dough begins to come together, then knead with your hands until it leaves the side of the bowl. Turn out on to a lightly floured surface and knead well for about 10 minutes, until smooth and elastic.

2 Brush a bowl with oil. Shape the dough into a ball, put it in the bowl and put the bowl into a plastic bag or cover with a damp tea towel. Leave to rise in a warm place for 1 hour, until the dough has doubled in volume.

3 Brush 2 baking sheets with oil. Turn out the dough on to a lightly floured surface and knock back with your fist. Divide it into 8 equal pieces, shape each into a ball and put them on the prepared baking sheets. Flatten slightly with a lightly floured hand and put the baking sheets into plastic bags or cover with damp tea towels. Leave to rise in a warm place for 30 minutes.

4 Preheat the oven to 200°C/400°F/Gas Mark 6. Lightly press the centre of each bun with your fingers to release any large air bubbles. Brush the tops with the oil and sprinkle with sesame seeds. Bake for 15–20 minutes, until light golden brown. Transfer to wire racks to cool.

gourmet bread

banana & orange bread

Ingredients

500 g/1 lb 2 oz strong white bread flour, plus an extra 1–3 tbsp for sticky dough and for dusting

1 tsp salt

1 tsp brown sugar

1 tsp easy-blend dried yeast

40 g/1½ oz butter, diced

2 medium ripe bananas or 1 large ripe banana, peeled and mashed

3 tbsp clear honey

4 tbsp orange juice

200 ml/7 fl oz lukewarm buttermilk or water

1½ tbsp skimmed milk powder (if using water)

sunflower oil, for greasing

milk, to glaze (optional)

MAKES 1 MEDIUM LOAF

1 Place the flour, salt, sugar and yeast in a large bowl. Rub in the butter and add the mashed bananas and honey. Make a well in the centre and gradually work in the orange juice, and the buttermilk or water, to make a smooth dough. If using water, add the skimmed milk powder to the mixture.

2 Turn the dough out on to a lightly floured surface and knead for 5–7 minutes, or until the dough is smooth and elastic. If the dough looks very sticky, add a further 1–2 tablespoons of white bread flour. (The stickiness depends on the ripeness and size of the bananas.) Brush a bowl with oil. Shape the dough into a ball, place it in the bowl and put the bowl into a plastic bag or cover with a damp tea towel. Leave to rise in a warm place for 1 hour, until the dough has doubled in volume.

3 Oil a 900-g/2-lb loaf tin. Turn the dough out on to a lightly floured work surface and knead for 1 minute until smooth. Shape the dough the length of the tin and three times the width. Fold the dough into three lengthways and place it in the tin with the join underneath. Cover and leave in a warm place for 30 minutes until it has risen above the tin.

4 Preheat the oven to 220°C/425°F/Gas Mark 7. Just before baking, brush the milk over the loaf to glaze, if desired.

5 Bake in the oven for 30 minutes, or until the loaf is firm and golden brown. Test that the loaf is cooked by tapping on the base with your knuckles – it should sound hollow. Transfer to a wire rack to cool.

orange marmalade loaf

Ingredients

450 g/1 lb strong white bread flour, plus extra for dusting

1¹/₂ tsp salt

1¹/₂ tsp caster sugar

1¹/₂ tsp easy-blend dried yeast

150 ml/5 fl oz lukewarm water

150 ml/5 fl oz lukewarm milk

2 tbsp vegetable oil, plus extra for brushing

7 tbsp orange marmalade

topping

1 egg yolk

1 tbsp milk

1 tbsp caster sugar

1–2 tbsp crystallized orange peel

MAKES 1 LOAF

1 Sift the flour and salt together into a bowl and stir in the sugar and yeast. Make a well in the centre and pour in the lukewarm water, milk and vegetable oil. Stir well with a wooden spoon until the dough begins to come together, then knead with your hands until it leaves the side of the bowl. Turn out on to a lightly floured surface and knead well for about 10 minutes, until smooth and elastic.

2 Brush a bowl with oil. Shape the dough into a ball, place it in the bowl and put the bowl into a plastic bag or cover with a damp tea towel. Leave to rise in a warm place for 1 hour, until the dough has doubled in volume.

3 Brush a 19 x 12 x 9 cm/7¹/₂ x 4¹/₂ x 3¹/₂ in loaf tin with oil. Turn out the dough on to a lightly floured surface and knock back with your fist. Roll out to a rectangle about 2 cm/³/₄ in thick. Spread the marmalade evenly over the dough leaving a 1-cm/¹/₂-in border along one long side. Roll up the dough like a Swiss roll and put it into the prepared tin, seam side down. Put the tin into a plastic bag or cover with a damp tea towel and leave to rise in a warm place for 45 minutes.

4 Preheat the oven to 220°C/425°F/Gas Mark 7. To make the topping, beat the egg yolk with the milk and sugar in a bowl and brush it over the top of the loaf. Score the top and sprinkle with the orange peel. Bake for 25–30 minutes, until golden brown. Transfer to a wire rack to cool.

muesli bread

Ingredients

300 g/10½ oz strong white bread flour, plus extra for dusting

85 g/3 oz strong wholemeal bread flour

1½ tsp salt

150 g/5½ oz unsweetened muesli

3 tbsp skimmed milk powder

1½ tsp easy-blend dried yeast

250 ml/8 fl oz lukewarm water

2 tbsp vegetable oil, plus extra for brushing

1 tbsp clear honey

70 g/2½ oz ready-to-eat dried apricots, chopped

MAKES 1 LOAF

1 Sift both types of flour and the salt together into a bowl and tip in the bran from the sieve. Stir in the muesli, milk powder and yeast. Make a well in the centre and pour in the lukewarm water, oil and honey. Stir well with a wooden spoon until the dough begins to come together, then knead with your hands until it leaves the side of the bowl. Turn out on to a lightly floured surface and knead well for 5 minutes. Knead in the apricots and continue to knead for a further 5 minutes, until the dough is smooth and elastic.

2 Brush a bowl with oil. Shape the dough into a ball, put it in the bowl and put the bowl into a plastic bag or cover with a damp tea towel. Leave to rise in a warm place for 1 hour, until the dough has doubled in volume.

3 Brush a baking sheet with oil. Turn out the dough on to a lightly floured surface and knock back with your fist. With lightly floured hands, shape the dough into a round and place on the prepared baking sheet. Cut a cross in the top of the loaf. Put the baking sheet into a plastic bag or cover with a damp tea towel and leave to rise in a warm place for 30–40 minutes.

4 Preheat the oven to 200°C/400°F/Gas Mark 6. Bake the loaf for 30–35 minutes, until golden brown and it sounds hollow when tapped on the base with your knuckles. Transfer to a wire rack to cool.

ryebread

Ingredients

450 g/1 lb rye flour

225 g/8 oz strong white bread flour, plus extra for dusting

2 tsp salt

2 tsp soft brown sugar

1½ tsp easy-blend dried yeast

425 ml/15 fl oz lukewarm water

2 tsp vegetable oil, plus extra for brushing

1 egg white

MAKES 1 LARGE LOAF

1 Sift the flours and salt together into a bowl. Add the sugar and yeast and stir to mix. Make a well in the centre and pour in the lukewarm water and oil. Stir with a wooden spoon until the dough begins to come together, then knead with your hands until it leaves the side of the bowl. Turn out on to a lightly floured surface and knead for 10 minutes, until elastic and smooth.

2 Brush a bowl with oil. Shape the dough into a ball, put it in the bowl and put the bowl in a plastic bag or cover with a damp tea towel. Leave to rise in a warm place for 2 hours, until the dough has doubled in volume.

3 Brush a baking sheet with oil. Turn out the dough on to a lightly floured surface and knock back with your fist, then knead for a further 10 minutes. Shape the dough into a ball, put it on the prepared baking sheet and put the baking sheet in a plastic bag or cover with a damp tea towel. Leave to rise in a warm place for a further 40 minutes, until the dough has doubled in volume.

4 Meanwhile, preheat the oven to 190°C/375°F/Gas Mark 5. Beat the egg white with 1 tbsp of water in a bowl. Bake the loaf for 20 minutes, then remove from the oven and brush the top with the egg white glaze. Return to the oven and bake for a further 20 minutes. Brush the top of the loaf with the glaze again and return to the oven for a further 20–30 minutes, until the crust is a rich brown colour and the loaf sounds hollow when tapped on the base with your knuckles. Transfer to a wire rack to cool.

cheesy granary bread

Ingredients

400 g/14 oz strong white bread flour, plus extra for dusting

55 g/2 oz granary flour

1 tsp salt

2 tsp sugar

1½ tsp easy-blend dried yeast

5 tbsp ricotta cheese, beaten

1 egg, lightly beaten

185 ml/6½ fl oz lukewarm water

85 g/3 oz Emmenthal cheese, grated

85 g/3 oz dolcelatte cheese, finely diced

3 tbsp finely chopped fresh chives

vegetable oil, for brushing

2 tbsp freshly grated Parmesan cheese

MAKES 1 LOAF

1 Sift both types of flour and the salt together into a bowl and stir in the sugar and yeast. Make a well in the centre and add the ricotta, egg and lukewarm water. Stir well with a wooden spoon until the dough begins to come together. Add the Emmenthal, dolcelatte and chives and knead with your hands until fully incorporated and the dough comes away from the side of the bowl. Turn out on to a lightly floured surface and knead well for about 10 minutes, until smooth and elastic.

2 Brush a bowl with oil. Shape the dough into a ball, put it in the bowl and put the bowl into a plastic bag or cover with a damp tea towel. Leave to rise in a warm place for 1 hour, until the dough has doubled in volume.

3 Brush a baking sheet with oil. Turn out the dough on to a lightly floured surface and knock back with your fist. With lightly floured hands, shape into a 20-cm/8-in round and place on the prepared baking sheet. Put the baking sheet into a plastic bag or cover with a damp tea towel and leave to rise in a warm place for 40–45 minutes.

4 Preheat the oven to 200°C/400°F/Gas Mark 6. Sprinkle the Parmesan over the loaf and bake for 40–45 minutes, until golden brown and it sounds hollow when tapped on the base with your knuckles. Transfer to a wire rack to cool.

plaited poppy seed bread

Ingredients

225 g/8 oz strong white bread flour, plus extra for dusting

1 tsp salt

2 tbsp skimmed milk powder

1½ tbsp caster sugar

1 tsp easy-blend dried yeast

175 ml/6 fl oz lukewarm water

2 tbsp vegetable oil, plus extra for brushing

5 tbsp poppy seeds

topping

1 egg yolk

1 tbsp milk

1 tbsp caster sugar

2 tbsp poppy seeds

MAKES 1 LOAF

1 Sift the flour and salt together into a bowl and stir in the milk powder, sugar and yeast. Make a well in the centre and pour in the lukewarm water and oil. Stir well with a wooden spoon until the dough begins to come together. Add the poppy seeds and knead with your hands until they are fully incorporated and the dough leaves the side of the bowl. Turn out on to a lightly floured surface and knead well for about 10 minutes, until smooth and elastic.

2 Brush a bowl with oil. Shape the dough into a ball, put it in the bowl and put the bowl into a plastic bag or cover with a damp tea towel. Leave to rise in a warm place for 1 hour, until the dough has doubled in volume.

3 Brush a baking sheet with oil. Turn out the dough on to a lightly floured surface, knock back with your fist and knead for 1–2 minutes. Divide the dough into 3 equal pieces and shape each into a rope 25–30 cm/10–12 in long.

4 Place the ropes side by side and press them together at one end. Plait the dough, pinch the other end together and tuck it underneath. Put the loaf on the prepared baking sheet. Put the baking sheet in a plastic bag or cover with a damp tea towel and leave to rise in a warm place for 30 minutes.

5 Preheat the oven to 200°C/400°F/Gas Mark 6. To make the topping, beat the egg yolk with the milk and sugar. Brush the egg glaze over the top of the loaf and sprinkle with the poppy seeds. Bake for 30–35 minutes, until golden brown and the loaf sounds hollow when tapped on the base with your knuckles. Transfer to a wire rack to cool.

pitta breads

Ingredients

350 g/12 oz strong white bread flour, plus extra for dusting

1½ tsp salt

1 tsp caster sugar

1 tsp easy-blend dried yeast

1 tbsp olive oil, plus extra for brushing

200 ml/7 fl oz lukewarm water

MAKES 6–8 PITTA BREADS

1 Sift the flour and salt together into a bowl and stir in the sugar and yeast. Make a well in the centre and pour in the oil and lukewarm water. Stir well with a wooden spoon until the dough begins to come together, then knead with your hands until it leaves the side of the bowl. Turn out on to a lightly floured surface and knead well for about 10 minutes, until smooth and elastic.

2 Brush a bowl with oil. Shape the dough into a ball, put it in the bowl and put the bowl into a plastic bag or cover with a damp tea towel. Leave to rise in a warm place for 1 hour, until the dough has doubled in volume.

3 Turn out on to a lightly floured surface and knock back with your fist. Divide the dough into 6 to 8 equal pieces, shape each piece into a ball and place on a tray. Put the tray into a plastic bag or cover with a damp tea towel and leave to rest for 10 minutes.

4 With floured hands, slightly flatten a dough ball and roll out on a lightly floured surface to an oval about 15 cm/6 in long and 5 mm/¼ in thick. Place on a lightly floured tea towel, sprinkle lightly with flour and cover with another tea towel. Repeat with the remaining dough balls and leave to rise for 30 minutes.

5 Meanwhile, put 2 or 3 baking sheets in the oven and preheat to 230°C/450°F/Gas Mark 8. Transfer the pitta breads to the heated baking sheets, spacing them well apart, and bake for 5 minutes, until puffed up and golden brown. Transfer to wire racks to cool slightly, then cover with a tea towel to keep them soft.

regional bread

ciabatta

Ingredients

400 ml/14 fl oz lukewarm water

4 tbsp lukewarm semi-skimmed milk

500 g/1 lb 2 oz strong white bread flour

1 sachet easy-blend dried yeast

2 tsp salt

3 tbsp olive oil

biga

350 g/12 oz strong white bread flour, plus extra for dusting

1¼ tsp easy-blend dried yeast

200 ml/7 fl oz lukewarm water

MAKES 3 LOAVES

1 First, make the biga. Sift the flour into a bowl, stir in the yeast and make a well in the centre. Pour in the lukewarm water and stir until the dough comes together. Turn out on to a lightly floured surface and knead for 5 minutes, until smooth and elastic. Shape the dough into a ball, put it in a bowl and put the bowl into a plastic bag or cover with a damp tea towel. Leave to rise in a warm place for 12 hours, until just beginning to collapse.

2 Gradually mix the water and milk into the biga, beating with a wooden spoon. Gradually mix in the flour and yeast with your hand, adding them a little at a time. Finally, mix in the salt and oil. The dough will be very wet; do not add extra flour. Put the bowl in a plastic bag or cover with a damp tea towel and leave to rise in a warm place for 2 hours, until the dough has doubled in volume.

3 Dust 3 baking sheets with flour. Using a spatula, divide the dough among the prepared baking sheets without knocking out the air. With lightly floured hands, gently pull and shape each piece of dough into a rectangular loaf, then flatten slightly. Dust the tops of the loaves with flour and leave to rise in a warm place for 30 minutes.

4 Meanwhile, preheat the oven to 220°C/425°F/Gas Mark 7. Bake the loaves for 25–30 minutes, until the crust is lightly golden and they sound hollow when tapped on the base with your knuckles. Transfer to wire racks to cool.

french baguettes

Ingredients

450 g/1 lb strong white bread flour, plus extra for dusting

1½ tsp salt

1½ tsp easy-blend dried yeast

325 ml/11 fl oz lukewarm water

vegetable oil, for brushing

MAKES 2 LOAVES

1 Sift the flour and salt together into a bowl and stir in the yeast. Make a well in the centre and pour in the lukewarm water. Stir well with a wooden spoon until the dough begins to come together, then knead with your hands until it leaves the side of the bowl. Turn out on to a lightly floured surface and knead well for about 10 minutes, until smooth and elastic.

2 Brush a bowl with oil. Shape the dough into a ball, put it in the bowl and put the bowl into a plastic bag or cover with a damp tea towel. Leave to rise in a warm place for 1 hour, until the dough has doubled in volume.

3 Turn out the dough on to a lightly floured surface, knock back with your fist and knead for 1–2 minutes. Cut the dough in half and shape each piece into a ball. Roll out each ball to a rectangle measuring 7.5 x 20 cm/3 x 8 in. From one long side of a dough rectangle, fold one-third of the dough down, then fold over the remaining third of the dough. Press gently. Fold the second dough rectangle in the same way. Put both loaves in plastic bags or cover with damp tea towels and leave to rest for 10 minutes. Repeat the rolling and folding twice more, leaving the dough to rest for 10 minutes each time.

4 Lightly flour and pleat 2 tea towels or flour 2 bannetons (lined French bread baskets). Gently roll and stretch each piece of dough until it is 30 cm/12 in long and an even thickness. Support each loaf on the pleated tea towels or in the bannetons, cover with damp tea towels and leave to rise for 30–40 minutes.

5 Preheat the oven to 230°C/450°F/Gas Mark 8. Brush 1 or 2 baking sheets with oil. Carefully roll the loaves on to the baking sheets and slash the tops several times with a sharp knife. Spray the oven with water (see page 10) and bake the loaves for 15–20 minutes, until golden brown. Transfer to a wire rack to cool.

olive & sun-dried tomato bread

Ingredients

400 g/14 oz plain flour, plus extra for dusting

1 tsp salt

1 sachet easy-blend dried yeast

1 tsp brown sugar

1 tbsp chopped fresh thyme

200 ml/7 fl oz lukewarm water

4 tbsp olive oil, plus extra for brushing

55 g/2 oz black olives, stoned and sliced

55 g/2 oz green olives, stoned and sliced

100 g/3½ oz sun-dried tomatoes in oil, drained and sliced

1 egg yolk, beaten

MAKES 2 LOAVES

1 Sift the flour and salt together into a bowl and stir in the yeast, sugar and thyme. Make a well in the centre and pour in the lukewarm water and olive oil. Stir well with a wooden spoon until the dough begins to come together, then knead with your hands until it leaves the side of the bowl. Turn out on to a lightly floured surface and knead in the olives and sun-dried tomatoes, then knead for a further 5 minutes, until the dough is smooth and elastic.

2 Brush a bowl with oil. Shape the dough into a ball, put it in the bowl and put the bowl into a plastic bag or cover with a damp tea towel. Leave to rise in a warm place for 1–1½ hours, until the dough has doubled in volume.

3 Dust a baking sheet with flour. Turn out the dough on to a lightly floured surface and knock back with your fist. Cut it in half and with lightly floured hands, shape each half into a round or oval. Put them on the prepared baking sheet and put the baking sheet into a plastic bag or cover with a damp tea towel. Leave to rise in a warm place for 45 minutes.

4 Preheat the oven to 200°C/400°F/Gas Mark 6. Make 3 shallow diagonal slashes on the top of each loaf and brush with the beaten egg yolk. Bake for 40 minutes, until golden brown and the loaves sound hollow when tapped on the base with your knuckles. Transfer to a wire rack to cool.

flatbread with onion & rosemary

Ingredients

450 g/1 lb strong white bread flour, plus extra for dusting

½ tsp salt

1½ tsp easy-blend dried yeast

2 tbsp chopped fresh rosemary, plus small sprigs to garnish

5 tbsp extra virgin olive oil, plus extra for brushing

300 ml/10 fl oz lukewarm water

1 red onion, thinly sliced and pushed out into rings

1 tbsp coarse sea salt

MAKES 1 LOAF

1 Sift the flour and salt together into a bowl and stir in the yeast and rosemary. Make a well in the centre and pour in 3 tbsp of the olive oil and the lukewarm water. Stir well with a wooden spoon until the dough begins to come together, then knead with your hands until it leaves the side of the bowl. Turn out on to a lightly floured surface and knead well for about 10 minutes, until smooth and elastic.

2 Brush a bowl with oil. Shape the dough into a ball, put it in the bowl and put the bowl into a plastic bag or cover with a damp tea towel. Leave to rise in a warm place for 1 hour, until the dough has doubled in volume.

3 Brush a baking sheet with oil. Turn out the dough on to a lightly floured surface, knock back with your fist and knead for 1 minute. Roll out the dough to a round about 30 cm/12 inches in diameter and put it on the prepared baking sheet. Put the baking sheet into a plastic bag or cover with a damp tea towel and leave to rise in a warm place for 20–30 minutes.

4 Preheat the oven to 200°C/400°F/Gas Mark 6. Using the handle of a wooden spoon, make indentations all over the surface of the loaf. Spread the onion rings over the top, drizzle with the remaining oil and sprinkle with the sea salt. Bake for 20 minutes. Sprinkle with the rosemary sprigs, return to the oven and bake for a further 5 minutes, until golden brown. Transfer to a wire rack to cool slightly and serve warm.

coriander & garlic naan

Ingredients

280 g/10 oz strong white bread flour, plus extra for dusting

1 tsp salt

1 tbsp ground coriander

1 garlic clove, very finely chopped

1 tsp easy-blend dried yeast

2 tsp clear honey

100 ml/3½ fl oz lukewarm water

4 tbsp natural yogurt

1 tbsp vegetable oil, plus extra for brushing

1 tsp black onion seeds

1 tbsp chopped fresh coriander

MAKES 3 NAAN

1 Sift the flour, salt and ground coriander together into a bowl and stir in the garlic and yeast. Make a well in the centre and pour in the honey, lukewarm water, yogurt and vegetable oil. Stir well with a wooden spoon until the dough begins to come together, then knead with your hands until it leaves the side of the bowl. Turn out on to a lightly floured surface and knead well for about 10 minutes, until smooth and elastic.

2 Brush a bowl with oil. Shape the dough into a ball, put it in the bowl and put the bowl into a plastic bag or cover with a damp tea towel. Leave to rise in a warm place for 1–2 hours, until the dough has doubled in volume.

3 Put 3 baking sheets into the oven and preheat to 240°C/475°F/Gas Mark 9. Preheat the grill. Turn out the dough on to a lightly floured surface and knock back with your fist. Divide the dough into 3 pieces, shape each piece into a ball and cover 2 of them with oiled clingfilm. Roll out the uncovered piece of dough into a teardrop shape about 8 mm/³/8 in thick and cover with oiled clingfilm. Roll out the other pieces of dough in the same way. Place the flatbreads on the hot baking sheets and sprinkle with the onion seeds and chopped coriander. Bake for 5 minutes, until puffed up. Transfer the naan bread to the grill pan, brush with oil and grill for 2–3 minutes. Serve warm.

greek olive & feta bread

Ingredients

375 g/13 oz strong white bread flour, plus extra for dusting

1 tsp salt

1½ tsp caster sugar

1 tbsp skimmed milk powder

1 tsp easy-blend dried yeast

200 ml/7 fl oz lukewarm water

55 g/2 oz stoned black olives, chopped

55 g/2 oz feta cheese, crumbled

2 tbsp olive oil, plus extra for brushing

1 tsp chopped fresh thyme

½ tsp dried oregano

MAKES 1 LOAF

1 Sift the flour and salt together into a bowl and stir in the sugar, milk powder and yeast. Make a well in the centre and pour in the lukewarm water. Stir well with a wooden spoon until the dough begins to come together, then knead with your hands until it leaves the side of the bowl. Turn out on to a lightly floured surface and knead in the olives and feta, then knead for a further 5 minutes, until the dough is smooth and elastic.

2 Brush a bowl with oil. Shape the dough into a ball, put it in the bowl and put the bowl into a plastic bag or cover with a damp tea towel. Leave to rise in a warm place for 1 hour, until the dough has doubled in volume.

3 Brush a 20-cm/8-in round cake tin with oil. Turn out the dough on a lightly floured surface and knock back with your fist. With lightly floured hands, shape it into a 20-cm/8-in round loaf and put it into the prepared tin. Put the tin into a plastic bag or cover with a damp tea towel and leave to rise in a warm place for 40–45 minutes.

4 Preheat the oven to 200°C/400°F/Gas Mark 6. Brush the top of the loaf with the olive oil and sprinkle with the herbs. Bake for 35–40 minutes, until golden brown. Turn out on to a wire rack to cool.

garlic & sage bread

Ingredients

250 g/9 oz strong brown bread flour, plus extra for dusting

1 sachet easy-blend dried yeast

3 tbsp chopped fresh sage

2 tsp sea salt

3 garlic cloves, finely chopped

1 tsp clear honey

150 ml/5 fl oz lukewarm water

vegetable oil, for brushing

MAKES 1 LOAF

1 Sift the flour into a bowl and tip in the bran from the sieve. Stir in the yeast, sage and half the sea salt. Reserve 1 tsp of the garlic and stir the remainder into the bowl. Make a well in the centre and pour in the honey and lukewarm water. Stir well with a wooden spoon until the dough begins to come together, then knead with your hands until it leaves the side of the bowl. Turn out on to a lightly floured surface and knead well for about 10 minutes, until smooth and elastic.

2 Brush a bowl with oil. Shape the dough into a ball, put it in the bowl and put the bowl into a plastic bag or cover with a damp tea towel. Leave to rise in a warm place for 1 hour, until the dough has doubled in volume.

3 Brush a baking sheet with oil. Turn out the dough on to a lightly floured surface, knock back with your fist and knead for 2 minutes. Roll the dough into a long sausage, shape into a ring and put it on to the prepared baking sheet. Brush the outside of a bowl with oil and put it into the centre of the ring to prevent it from closing up while the dough is rising. Put the baking sheet into a plastic bag or cover with a damp tea towel and leave to rise in a warm place for 30 minutes.

4 Preheat the oven to 200°C/400°F/Gas Mark 6. Remove the bowl from the centre of the loaf. Sprinkle the loaf with the remaining sea salt and the reserved garlic and bake for 25–30 minutes, until golden brown and the loaf sounds hollow when tapped on the base with your knuckles. Transfer to a wire rack to cool.

cornbread

Ingredients

vegetable oil, for brushing
175 g/6 oz plain flour
1 tsp salt
4 tsp baking powder
1 tsp caster sugar
280 g/10 oz yellow cornmeal
115 g/4 oz butter, softened
4 eggs
250 ml/8 fl oz milk
3 tbsp double cream

MAKES 1 SMALL LOAF

1 Preheat the oven to 200°C/400°F/Gas Mark 6. Brush a 20-cm/8-in square cake tin with oil.

2 Sift the flour, salt and baking powder together into a bowl. Add the sugar and cornmeal and stir to mix. Add the butter and cut it into the dry ingredients with a knife, then rub in with your fingertips until the mixture resembles breadcrumbs.

3 Lightly beat the eggs in a bowl with the milk and cream, then stir into the cornmeal mixture until thoroughly combined.

4 Spoon the mixture into the prepared tin and smooth the surface. Bake for 30–35 minutes, until a wooden cocktail stick inserted into the centre of the loaf comes out clean. Remove the tin from the oven and leave to cool for 5–10 minutes, then cut into squares and serve warm.

basic pizza dough

Ingredients

175 g/6 oz plain flour, plus extra for dusting

1 tsp salt

1 tsp easy-blend dried yeast

1 tbsp olive oil, plus extra for brushing and drizzling

6 tbsp lukewarm water

topping

175 ml/6 fl oz ready-made pizza tomato sauce or 350 g/ 12 oz tomatoes, peeled and halved

1 garlic clove, thinly sliced

55 g/2 oz mozzarella cheese, thinly sliced

1 tsp dried oregano

sprigs of fresh basil, to garnish

salt and pepper

MAKES 1 PIZZA

1 Sift the flour and salt together into a bowl and stir in the yeast. Make a well in the centre and pour in the oil and lukewarm water. Stir well with a wooden spoon until the dough begins to come together, then knead with your hands until it leaves the side of the bowl. Turn out on to a lightly floured surface and knead well for 5–10 minutes, until smooth and elastic.

2 Brush a bowl with oil. Shape the dough into a ball, put it in the bowl and put the bowl into a plastic bag or cover with a damp tea towel. Leave to rise in a warm place for 1 hour, until the dough has doubled in volume.

3 Brush a baking sheet with oil. Turn out the dough on to a lightly floured surface, knock back with your fist and knead for 1 minute. Roll or press out the dough to a 25-cm/10-in round. Place on the prepared baking sheet and push up the edge slightly all round. Put the baking sheet in a plastic bag or cover with a damp tea towel and leave to rise in a warm place for 10 minutes.

4 Preheat the oven to 200°C/400°F/Gas Mark 6. Spread the tomato sauce if using, over the pizza base almost to the edge. If using fresh tomatoes, squeeze out some of the juice and coarsely chop the flesh. Spread them evenly over the pizza base and drizzle with olive oil. Sprinkle the garlic over the tomato, add the mozzarella, sprinkle with the oregano and season with salt and pepper. Bake for 15–20 minutes, until the crust is golden brown and crisp. Brush the crust with olive oil, garnish with basil and serve immediately.

turkish flatbread

Ingredients

750 g/1 lb 10 oz plain flour, plus extra for dusting

1½ tsp salt

1 tsp ground cumin

½ tsp ground coriander

1 tsp caster sugar

1 sachet easy-blend dried yeast

2 tbsp olive oil, plus extra for brushing

400 ml/14 fl oz lukewarm water

MAKES 8 FLATBREAD

1 Sift the flour, salt, cumin and coriander together into a bowl and stir in the sugar and yeast. Make a well in the centre and pour in the olive oil and lukewarm water. Stir well with a wooden spoon until the dough begins to come together, then knead with your hands until it leaves the side of the bowl. Turn out on to a lightly floured surface and knead well for about 10 minutes, until smooth and elastic.

2 Brush a bowl with oil. Shape the dough into a ball, put it in the bowl and put the bowl into a plastic bag or cover with a damp tea towel. Leave to rise in a warm place for 1 hour, until the dough has doubled in volume.

3 Lightly brush a baking sheet with oil. Turn out the dough on to a lightly floured surface, knock back with your fist and knead for 1–2 minutes. Divide the dough into 8 equal pieces, shape each piece into a ball, then roll out to a 20-cm/8-in round. Cover the rounds with a damp tea towel and leave to rest for 20 minutes.

4 Heat a heavy-based frying pan and brush the base with oil. Add 1 dough round, cover and cook for 2–3 minutes, until lightly browned on the underside. Turn over with a fish slice, re-cover the pan and cook for a further 2 minutes, until lightly browned on the second side. Remove from the pan and cook the remaining dough rounds in the same way.

sweet bread

banana & cranberry loaf

Ingredients

butter, for greasing
215 g/7½ oz self-raising flour
½ tsp baking powder
125 g/4½ oz soft brown sugar
2 bananas, mashed
55 g/2 oz chopped mixed peel
85 g/3 oz chopped mixed nuts
40 g/1½ oz dried cranberries
5–6 tbsp orange juice
2 eggs, lightly beaten
150 ml/5 fl oz vegetable oil
85 g/3 oz icing sugar
grated rind of 1 orange

MAKES 1 LOAF

1 Preheat the oven to 180°C/350°F/Gas Mark 4. Grease a 900-g/ 2-lb loaf tin with butter and line the base with baking parchment.

2 Sift the flour and baking powder together into a bowl and stir in the sugar, bananas, mixed peel, nuts and cranberries. Mix the orange juice, eggs and oil together in another bowl, then add to the dry ingredients. Stir well with a wooden spoon until thoroughly combined.

3 Spoon the mixture into the prepared loaf tin and smooth the top. Bake for 1 hour, until golden and firm and a cocktail stick inserted into the centre of the loaf comes out clean. Turn out on to a wire rack to cool.

4 Mix the icing sugar with a little water in a bowl and drizzle it over the cooled loaf. Sprinkle the orange rind on top and leave to set.

pecan honey tea bread

Ingredients

500 g/1 lb 2 oz strong white bread flour, plus extra for dusting

3/4 tbsp salt

1 1/2 tsp easy-blend dried yeast

40 g/1 1/2 oz unsalted butter

40 g/1 1/2 oz pecan nuts, chopped

1 tbsp grated orange rind

125 ml/4 fl oz lukewarm milk

175 ml/6 fl oz mandarin or orange yogurt

3 tbsp clear honey

vegetable oil, for brushing

MAKES 1 LOAF

1 Sift the flour and salt together into a bowl and stir in the yeast. Add the butter and rub in with your fingertips, then stir in the nuts and orange rind. Make a well in the centre and pour in the lukewarm milk, yogurt and honey. Stir well with a wooden spoon until the dough begins to come together, then knead with your hands until it leaves the side of the bowl. Turn out on to a lightly floured surface and knead well for about 10 minutes, until smooth and elastic.

2 Brush a bowl with oil. Shape the dough into a ball, put it in the bowl and put the bowl into a plastic bag or cover with a damp tea towel. Leave to rise in a warm place for 1 hour, until the dough has doubled in volume.

3 Brush a 900-g/2-lb loaf tin with oil. Turn out the dough on to a lightly floured surface, knock back with your fist and knead for 1 minute. With lightly floured hands, flatten the dough into a rectangle the same width as the tin. Fold it into 3 and place in the prepared tin, seam side down. Put the tin into a plastic bag or cover with a damp tea towel and leave to rise in a warm place for 30–40 minutes, until the dough has reached the top of the tin.

4 Meanwhile, preheat the oven to 230°C/450°F/Gas Mark 8. Bake the loaf for 30–40 minutes, until it has shrunk from the sides of the tin, the crust is golden brown and it sounds hollow when tapped on the base with your knuckles. Turn out on to a wire rack to cool.

malted fruit loaf

Ingredients

350 g/12 oz plain flour, plus extra for dusting

1 tsp salt

1 tsp easy-blend dried yeast

140 g/5 oz sultanas

200 ml/7 fl oz lukewarm water

2 tsp vegetable oil, plus extra for brushing

2 tbsp malt extract

1½ tbsp treacle

MAKES 1 LOAF

1 Sift the flour and salt together into a bowl and stir in the yeast and sultanas. Make a well in the centre and pour in the lukewarm water, vegetable oil, malt extract and treacle. Stir well with a wooden spoon until the dough begins to come together, then knead with your hands until it leaves the side of the bowl. Turn out on to a lightly floured surface and knead well for about 10 minutes, until smooth and elastic.

2 Brush a bowl with oil. Shape the dough into a ball, put it in the bowl and put the bowl into a plastic bag or cover with a damp tea towel. Leave to rise in a warm place for 1–2 hours, until the dough has doubled in volume.

3 Brush a 900-g/2 lb loaf tin with oil. Turn out the dough on to a lightly floured surface, knock back with your fist and knead for 1 minute. With lightly floured hands, flatten the dough into a rectangle the same width as the tin. Fold it into 3 and place in the prepared tin, seam side down. Put the tin into a plastic bag or cover with a damp tea towel and leave to rise in a warm place for 30–40 minutes, until the dough has reached the top of the tin.

4 Meanwhile, preheat the oven to 230°C/450°F/Gas Mark 8. Bake the loaf for 30–40 minutes, until it has shrunk from the sides of the tin, the crust is golden brown and it sounds hollow when tapped on the base with your knuckles. Turn out on to a wire rack to cool.

apple & apricot tea loaf

Ingredients

115 g/4 oz unsalted butter, softened, plus extra for greasing

150 g/5½ oz brown sugar

2 eggs, lightly beaten

70 g/2½ oz ready-to-eat dried apricots, chopped

2 eating apples, peeled, cored and coarsely grated

2 tbsp milk

175 g/6 oz self-raising flour

1 tsp ground allspice

½ tsp ground cinnamon

MAKES 1 LOAF

1 Preheat the oven to 180°C/350°F/Gas Mark 4. Grease a 900-g/2-lb loaf tin with butter and line with baking parchment.

2 Cream the butter and sugar together in a bowl until light and fluffy. Gradually beat in the eggs. Reserve 1 tbsp of the apricots and fold in the remainder with the apples and milk. Sift the flour, allspice and cinnamon together into the bowl and fold into the mixture.

3 Spoon the mixture into the prepared tin and sprinkle the reserved apricots on top. Bake for 55–60 minutes, until risen and golden and a cocktail stick inserted into the centre comes out clean. Leave to cool in the tin for 10 minutes, then turn on to a wire rack, and leave to cool completely.

devonshire splits

Ingredients

225 g/8 oz strong white bread flour, plus extra for dusting

½ tsp salt

2 tbsp caster sugar

1 tsp easy-blend dried yeast

150 ml/5 fl oz lukewarm water

1 tbsp melted butter

vegetable oil, for brushing

icing sugar, for dusting

filling

strawberry jam

clotted cream or stiffly whipped double cream

MAKES 8 SPLITS

1 Sift the flour and salt together into a bowl and stir in the caster sugar and yeast. Make a well in the centre and pour in the lukewarm water and melted butter. Stir well with a wooden spoon until the dough begins to come together, then knead with your hands until it leaves the side of the bowl. Turn out on to a lightly floured surface and knead well for about 10 minutes, until smooth and elastic.

2 Brush a bowl with oil. Shape the dough into a ball, put it in the bowl and put the bowl into a plastic bag or cover with a damp tea towel. Leave to rise in a warm place for 1–1½ hours, until the dough has doubled in volume.

3 Brush 2 baking sheets with oil. Turn out the dough on to a lightly floured surface and knock back with your fist. Divide the dough into 8 equal pieces, shape each piece into a ball, put them on to the prepared baking sheets and flatten slightly. Put the baking sheets into plastic bags or cover with damp tea towels and leave to rise in a warm place for 45 minutes.

4 Preheat the oven to 220°C/425°F/Gas Mark 7. Bake the buns for 15 minutes, until golden. Transfer to a wire rack to cool completely. To serve, split in half with a sharp knife, spread the bottom half with plenty of strawberry jam and top with a good spoonful of cream. Replace the tops, dust lightly with icing sugar and serve.

gingerbread

Ingredients

150 g/5½ oz butter, plus extra for greasing

175 g/6 oz soft brown sugar

2 tbsp treacle

2 eating apples

1 tbsp lemon juice

225 g/8 oz plain flour

1 tsp baking powder

2 tsp bicarbonate of soda

2 tsp ground ginger

150 ml/5 fl oz milk

1 egg, lightly beaten

MAKES 12 BARS

1 Preheat the oven to 160°C/325°F/Gas Mark 3. Grease a 23-cm/9-in square cake tin with butter and line with baking parchment.

2 Put the butter, sugar and treacle into a saucepan and melt over a low heat, stirring occasionally. Remove the pan from the heat and leave to cool.

3 Meanwhile, peel, core and chop the apples, then toss in a bowl with the lemon juice and set aside. Sift the flour, baking powder, bicarbonate of soda and ground ginger into another bowl. Make a well in the centre, add the milk, egg and cooled butter mixture and stir with a wooden spoon until thoroughly combined. Stir in the chopped apple.

4 Pour the mixture into the prepared tin and smooth the surface. Bake for 30–35 minutes, until the gingerbread has risen and a cocktail stick inserted into the centre comes out clean. Leave to cool in the tin before turning out and cutting into 12 bars.

italian chocolate chip bread

Ingredients

vegetable oil, for brushing

225 g/8 oz plain flour, plus extra for dusting

1 tbsp cocoa powder

pinch of salt

15 g/½ oz butter, plus ½ tsp melted butter for brushing

1 tbsp caster sugar

1 sachet easy-blend dried yeast

150 ml/5 fl oz lukewarm water

55 g/2 oz plain chocolate chips

MAKES 1 LOAF

1 Brush a baking sheet with oil. Sift the flour, cocoa powder and salt together into a bowl. Add the butter and cut it into the dry ingredients, then stir in the sugar and yeast.

2 Gradually add the lukewarm water, stirring well with a wooden spoon until the dough begins to come together, then knead with your hands until it leaves the side of the bowl. Turn out on to a lightly floured surface and knead for about 10 minutes, until smooth and elastic.

3 Knead the chocolate chips into the dough, then form into a round loaf. Put the loaf on to the prepared baking sheet and put the baking sheet into a plastic bag or cover with a damp tea towel. Leave to rise in a warm place for 1–1½ hours, until the dough has doubled in volume.

4 Preheat the oven to 220°C/425°F/Gas Mark 7. Bake the loaf for 10 minutes, then reduce the oven temperature to 190°C/375°F/Gas Mark 5 and bake for a further 15 minutes.

5 Transfer the loaf to a wire rack and brush the top with the melted butter. Cover with a tea towel and leave to cool.